WHAT THE KNIGHT BRINGS
BY SIR RODERICK E. BECTON II

What the knight brings with such poetic rings which make your heart soar and free.

What the knight brings that holds you captive in a trance that may open a feverish response of the body' desires.

To be held without love is like being captive in a tower such as a prisoner that will never be free unless truly freed by love in its self.

Such imprisonment is a punishment meant by a hand of malice and inflicted upon the unexpected.

To be freed from such is what the knight brings to hold only in the light of his heart the power to heal ones emptiness.

To only be seen but not heard when the reality of the pain that love exists no more then to turn to others only to place oneself into a false sense of perfection.

What the knight brings is the key to many towers that have imprisoned so many for a very long time.

THE END

A TAIL OF A BUNNY

BY SIR RODERICK E. BECTON II

A tail of a bunny is a greatly sweet thing to feel my joy swell while I hold your love dear to my heart.

A tail of a bunny is a very delicious taste to have her to hold her to shield her from all that harms.

A tail of a bunny oh how I yearn with desire to only hold myself deep within you to create a fire so intense that the entire world can see the brightness of the light.

A tail of a bunny if I were to be invited to feast I would protect you throughout my entire life and shield you with my love and pledge this to the heavens the earth and the universe.

A tail of a bunny I must end my tale only to place my heart in your fate with the hope that all will never be lost and that our love will always find each other.

THE END

GENTLE BREEZE

BY SIR RODERICK E. BECTON II

As something as gentle as the touch of my hand which makes all that glistens mine to have.

A gentle breeze is that from which whispers from my lips and makes your stomach yearn with desire.

When I pull you so close to the warmth that which my body creates I can only hope that the world will not shake apart and the gasp for which your voice creates is invitation to take you within my love.

A gentle breeze so gentle the kiss for which I have placed upon your lips with the hope that I create a moment in time which will never be forgotten.

A gentle breeze still blows lightly in the trees until the love that is desired is created to bask in each others love for eternity.

THE END

AS THE WIND

BY SIR RODERICK E. BECTON II

As the wind I am like the dragons breath that fuels your inner most desires opening the doors to the lust within your hear creating a moistness that I yearn to taste.

As the wind I am like a whisper that can be heard day or night waiting to come into the warmth of your heart to give you my love.

As the wind the moist touch of your lips makes my heart beat fierce with a fiery passion waiting to take you further into my life embracing you passionately within my arms.

As the wind I have longed to plunge myself deep into the love which I created with the sound of my voice thru my words and my passion within.

Only as the wind may I come into the night to taste your love and your lust which has fueled my desires and driven me past insanity only not to hold the one I truly desire which will forever be you.

THE END

BROWN TOWN

BY SIR RODERICK E. BECTON II

In brown town where I get down to hang all around being cool is where I can be found that is in brown town.

In brown town as cool as I can be the brothers hang with me while trying to see how the good sisters are to me that is in brown town.

In brown town when I feel like getting down I know where to go to find the soul mans flow that's where the lyrics grow in brown town.

As I flow to a rhyme in time where the lyrics still find me in good health while gathering back all my wealth that is in brown town. FREE STYLE BABY!

It seems like I can hear I mean the lyrics inside my ears while closing my eyes to my surprise the words are inside my mind I mean the kind that makes you flow out of control and wanting to rhyme being the kind and his grin oh what a grin that's in brown town.

I am the kind I have always been the kind to blow your minds I find the need to rhyme I mean of the free style money kind that is in brown town. CAN YOU DIG IT!

In brown town where my olive skin can be found hanging with all those who are cool. SEE YOU AROUND IN BROWN TOWN.

THE END

THE FIRE

BY SIR RODERICK E. BECTON II

The fire which fuels the desires that is within my heart which holds love so dear is a fiery that burns out of control.

The fire which burns so brightly that has touched so many lives that have secretly desired to be touched and held to a passions end.

As to touch and hold to devourer the one who truly deserves the earth as it shakes which represents my love for thee. Is this deemed the fire?

To know this and not to speak is this someone who has fell to love? Or is it that of someone who has imprisoned ones self to the miseries of life that is inevitable an emptiness which can not be filled by any other but that who brings true love.

Yet the fire burns on yearning to be held so its furry can be cherished and to have love live in existence.

THE END

SHAKE THE EARTH

BY SIR RODERICK E. BECTON II

What has come to the point when I shake the earth to awaken what once has roamed freely.

Is this to awaken those who have become the elements of time and entrusted to hold the keys?

Or is it to find ones way which has been clouded by others who only think smugly that they have fooled.

But could it be the essence of love seeping out to look but not find what others take for granted?

It must be! Then shake the earth and see if the angles above answer to my call and heal what is broken and find what is lost.

Then shake the earth to still all that is inside which yearns and hurts wanting to be held and loved until the earths end.

Then I shall shake the earth until my love for you is heard by all and only then will you understand my love.

THE END

MOODS OF LOVE
BY SIR RODERICK E. BECTON II

Moods of love by the power of three which will always be of great beauty. Does it run hot or cold fast or slow or does it seem to sit still.

Moods of love does it feel great to be alive or is it like being engulfed in your life to no end.

Moods of love does it make you walk on air or short of breath but at the same time your stomach aches to the point of pain without end.

Moods of love does it turn so dark that it seems to fade having you loose all hope that only you understand.

Moods of love is all of this and even more. The quest is to find the one whose moods of love overtake your turning points of darkness and enforces the passions and desires of love which brings back the joys of life and happiness.

THE END

IT STARTS WITH AN "M"

BY SIR RODERICK E. BECTON II

It starts with an "M". Is this someone who is magnificent to my mind or is it the doorway to my heart.

Is it the love of my life or the one who truly brings the air I breathe which enables life in itself?

It starts with an "M". Is this mine to have for most of my dreams that have came so true to find love as pure as this which made the entire world come to a stand still?

Is this the desire that is promised which most enjoy without thinking of the joys that have graced their lives which is now at my doorstep wanting to come in while my heart keeps throwing the doorway open so wide that it is perceived as destruction?

Is it the wind that I write of or the earth that has moved beneath me when I call her name breaking into sobs of despair when no answer is heard?

Is it to no end that I love her only to seeing pebbles in the pathway of love when all others see obstacles of determent?

It truly does start wit an "M" and it is my heart which I have mentioned and as my breath expels her name it says I truly do love you Mila.

THE END?

THE LIGHT

BY SIR RODERICK E. BECTON II

The light which has befriended is that of such that in name or title is a Prince which is of me.

That that is casted upon you by the light is that of love for which is only been tasted from a distance that's far away.

The light which has brought the sun to the sky only to light ones path for the hours in the day for which the light has existed until the light fades.

That that is warmed from the light is the heart which has left the earth once before which casted itself to the sky above. Was this in anger or did life just end.

In darkness comes all that brings to the night which can not exist in the light. Has time stood still or did all just end.

Always reach for the light which is the love and desires in the world today for in darkness he comes.

THE END

THE BAD MAN WILL COME

BY SIR RODERICK E. BECTON II

Call into the night which has dwelled for many years that of which I tell the tale of today.

Call into the night for this is where the BAD MAN exists and where his friends dwell as well.

For what has only existed in darkness now has come for all that has fell from the light. This darkness is now at the crest of what life itself has feared for many years.

The Bad Man Will Come for you to aid all of those that have been befriended by him and he walks with death at his side.

THE BEGINNING

WALK WITH ME

BY SIR RODERICK E. BECTON II

Walk with me to the side which has failed the love in my heart that now erupts with destruction.

For now there is no safety to hide behind and no one around that cares for you in the house that dwells that of the night.

For now you have awaken what you have sought after for so long that it is upon your breath like a name you commonly say in any given day.

For then you will see all that you have called upon in a destructive tone with smite and malice now willing to appear.

For that you will finally see what has been celebrated by some and feared by others only to come from the same breath which has brought life that now has taken your offering and brings you the death you desire.

Walk With Me and you will see who brings you the death you so much desire.

THE MIDDLE

WHO BRINGS DEATH

BY SIR RODERICK E. BECTON II

Who brings to you death that you can only whisper from lips that should not exist to remove all that has went bad.

Who brings death to remove the hardship which has broken all but in spirit which has known of this if from the same whisper.

Who comes from all that is light to bring the destruction that is celebrated in taste for all that has known of this existence.

Who brings to an end through death the results that are known but in today's world still embraced as that of the past.

Who brings life back to those who entrusted death to heal all that time has left broken through hardship and heartache.

Has death come only to return? Is this the question that faces so many of us today?

IN TIME

THE BOOGIE MAN

BY SIR RODERICK E. BECTON II

What now has slept undisturbed like a rock for which represents that which has been deemed soiled. NOW HAS ARISEN!

For what you have called for only if in ignorance has now been heard and now must be addressed.

For in this poem the verse is that which has become to be known as THE BOOGIE MAN.

I care not for your hearts that now I have spat upon numerous of times which to gaze at your souls I now laugh with delight at the appearance of what may not be known. THE BOOGIE MAN.

I stand no more the sounds of your voices for which I have heard many a time in response to what could have been. THE BOOGIE MAN.

I have only wept to the lost of love or when enraged to the point of your destruction then pulled the world back. THE BOOGIE MAN.

Now I have come to answer your call PLEASE BE AWARE THIS IS THE BOOGIE MAN!

THE END

LUSTY BREEZE

BY SIR RODERICK E. BECTON II

Lusty as the breeze is my breath that has heaved with passion to a point of blind desire.

Lusty as a breeze that has singled you out to have my way in the many positions of lust.

My lust has now grown stronger which has now turned to animal instinct ready to take your body and burn away your morals.

My lust is now past the point of not caring that you may have another. I am what you desired and I will have my way.

Now you know of what power I now posses over you and this has created a point of no return.

My passion is now heat my lust is now rising to come inside without knocking but just entering with the nod of your head I am now inside you which is HOT!

THE END

HOT!

BY SIR RODERICK E. BECTON II

Hot can be the time that all stood still to only capture the breath of someone special.

Hot can be a look of a motion which ignites oneself and excels them to an orbit which creates gravity.

Hot can be the woman of my dreams no matter how wet they become while my manhood grows with the anticipation of moistness that I have created within moments of a pulsating drive then spurting with exhaustion. NOW THAT'S HOT!

Hot are all that I have explained and more while I ask how you feel still inside you pumping feverishly to become one with you deep inside your love. IF ONLY FOR A KISS.

Now that is the love I have which can burn brightly as a star in the sky or a star within my eye which I hold dearly to my heart.

NOW THAT'S HOT!

THE END

TALES OF LOVE
BY SIR RODERICK E. BECTON II

Tales of love like a roller coaster in life hoping that there are more ups than downs.

Tales of love like the joy in your heart burning brightly as a fire lighting the path of love which is now found.

Tales of love has many verses that may make you laugh or cry live or want to die because love can create a void.

These are the things that tell the tales of love which can make the hurt go away.

THE END

WORDS

BY SIR RODERICK E. BECTON II

Words they are all around which can be filled with life and love song and rhyme to create the meanings desired.

To take these words and fill those as I which captures the heart and makes the soul soar to the highest points of delight which makes the appetite grow. Are these the words you seek?

Or to sour the life as the day that has just been put behind which was to the extremes of beyond the worst. Or are these the words you seek?

If I could make the day go greatly past what is normally expected even by your wildest dreams would this not make the basis of a friend or even your lover? Are these the words?

To lift what was once in shambles then resurrect it with the love which is in my heart only to ask for a kiss. Would not these words suffice?

To put words into action removing all that would hurt you to better equip you to life with what manufactures true love to the point that all related to your heart aches. This is what I ask.

WORDS!

LIFE AND LOVE

BY SIR RODERICK E. BECTON II

Life and love as spoken from words is the sweetest part of existence which can be embraced to a firry point of love.

To live ones' life with the ability to love only not yet to find but constantly seeking to the point of despair in life itself but without the product of love which is desired.

Now to fuel the desires with the fulfillment of love and to live ones' life embracing this true love is truly to live to your fullest potential and to be engulfed in love and the desires which loves brings.

Once this achievement is grasped even when you are so deeply in love that only bells are heard in the ringing of your ears can you say that life has become bearable and now I must truly live.

LIFE AND LOVE

THE END

HOW THE WORLD WORKS

BY SIR RODERICK E. BECTON II

How the world works with the products of love and hate never meant to conflict to a point beyond passion to create destruction. Shall I call?

How the world works to calm oneself once there is acknowledgement of what should have become only to find conflict and turmoil. Arrival inevitable.

How the world works to the point of joy that all is calmed by a hand that has been deemed beyond what could have been expected. Shall we dine?

How the world works with all that has been placed to create a moment in history which is spoken amongst ourselves. Now we enjoy.

How could the world work if certain things were ignored and a hand so calm was not to be found?

TO THE WORLD

FLOWER

BY SIR RODERICK E. BECTON II

Flower the beauty in the petals the smell and the touch to thane eyes of mine which has the scent of love about to cross my lips.

Such fragrance is to be tasted as life and love which lives hand in hand to become the beauty within the flower which is pleasing to the eye.

To blossom in bloom the beauty of fragranced love that can be tasted by lips which now I want to devour with the fire of my love.

To engulf the beauty of the flower that has petals like the rose wanting to savor not pluck but nourish the love which is the question that I ask but to also protect the flower with my love?

Is this question too complex to be answered yet can you explain why I shall always be in love with you for which my heart has erupted feverishly for you.

Such a flower exists and I shall have this flower as mine to become my garden for which I shall always embrace in love.

THE END

MAY I FILL YOUR CUP

BY SIR RODERICK E. BECTON II

May I fill your cup which I can hold in my hands with the warmth that now exists between us.

May I plunge my love deeply inside of you to a point of explosive reaction that may leave your body a quiver?

May I fill your cup with my tongue as juices flow to the point that now I have the taste of what my mouth has forever desired?

May I feverishly feast on what you bring to our bedroom now on my knees if not to beg but not?

May I fill your cup with my love as it pulsates to a point which aches my loins creating a feeling which alone brings all that is desired to what now glistens?

I have filled your cup and now I know what in life itself I have truly missed and my hunger now has grown for forever love.

THE END

HAS IT

BY SIR RODERICK E. BECTON II

Has it been so long ago that my rhymes have created a flow so pure that you now understand me.

Has it been to the point that it seems all has failed yet there is nothing left in our world but destruction? Yes destruction.

Well now's the time for a better yield to better ourselves even in the field that's for the players. Yes the players.

I have been called Don for some time ago which now is the time to create my team for those who know. That is called a leader. Yes a leader. They made me a leader.

Now is the time to rise to the top with the hustler's blessings I still having my knot. That means I have my money. Yes my money.

Back when I was just the hand of New York I had the chance to be a top. That is how I made it. Yes I made it.

Has it been an experience that only those who know in the corporate world I will always flow from my experience. Now you know.

THE END

LOVE

BY SIR RODERICK E. BECTON II

Love is the way your heart feels when everything that can go wrong does and I look to you and can still smile.

This is what the angles have brought from the heavens above to truly look into the heat of my passion and create a love so intense that the heavens above even feel hot with desire.

Love is the purity of two hearts that has a chemical reaction to create combustion that leads to marriage.

Love is not making any sense to anyone other than to the one whom you have created the connection with.

Love is the Cookie Monster and Grover covering all bases so you can play golf all day every day without leaving your home.

Love is crying for the one whom you love so much hoping that all is heard and is felt the same. That is what love is.

THE END

DAYS THAT PASS

BY SIR RODERICK E. BECTON II

Days that pass as do the feelings that I have for you wanting to keep the fire burning brightly I must love.

As you turned to me with a tear in your eye I finally understood the difference of our love.

As a man I feel strongly of my desires and very little of the matters of the heart which I have cherished for so long.

I have finally heard the small cry from your lips taking the time to create the love that you have desired for so long which this love has always existed in my heart and I now can voice as proudly as you.

The days that have passed have become a learning experience to love you until the end of time.

The days that have passed have closed the gaps between us as a couple which now has created an endless love.

The days that have passed have turned into passionate nights that are no longer spent alone fulfilled with desire fueling our love creating an eternal flame.

The days now that will pass are spent in a life so harmonic that even what once was bad will now good and our love has bonded forever in a eternal light.

THE END

NO MORE

BY SIR RODERICK E. BECTON II

No more lies to tell only that I have always loved you even from a far which was like death not able to hold or to touch or even to savior the taste of your lips.

No more vagueness of pretense that I have not a feeling of caring which is now fully blown and that the love I have for you rages with the passion of a thousand universes unfolding to create the desire within my heart.

No more distance when you ask me what is on my mind and I look away fearful to tell you of my secrets and of my desires.

No more sadness in my heart knowing that I may now open up freely showing you all my hearts desires and showing you the world that exists from now and until our eternal time forever together.

NO MORE

HEAT INTO THE NIGHT
BY SIR RODERICK E. BECTON II

Heat into the night to remember the one's that were and now have passed along as if they were still here today.

Heat into the night when times started so simple then through success created the hardships that friends are forever lost.

Heat into the night when my path was of differs and now thru time it has become quite evident that this course should exist to remove the pain that does not need existence.

To the heat of the night for all who know what true friendship is that can lead to the warmth of a family that is desired.

The night's heat can comfort even in trying times.

THE END

MY HEART

BY SIR RODERICK E. BECTON II

My heart is that of a thousand fires burning so brightly that all the heavens above can see seeking a better time for which created a light hearted laughter such as the time of Carol Burnett, Tim Conway, Vicky Lawrence and those friends for whom has passed.

My heart with the ability to touch tattered souls so tormented with anguish thus bringing them back to the levels of love.

My heart has not been but will shatter to the touch of what I deem true love. If not to be loved then what will be the warmth at least the laughter?

My heart which is not on my sleeve but in my chest to heal only the one who has the ability to hold candles which burn so brightly which has the intensity of a thousand suns. This is deemed my heart.

My heart has filled itself and it starts with "M".

THE END

HIS NAME WAS JINGLELAY

BY SIR RODERICK E. BECTON II

His name was Jinglelay or that was what it was that day he made so many people laugh and smile.

His name was that of many that he reenacted through his work of many years of pleasured fun through entertainment.

He would lean back and rub his chest with a smile saying jinglelay jinglelay with a few other words of choice that sound like trucker.

He has touched so many lives with his humor and his whit that it saddens me that in this life time we will never meet.

See you on the other side Bernie!

WITH LOVE THE END

CLAIMED BY THE SEA
BY SIR RODERICK E. BECTON II

This dangerous job that has claimed so many by the sea has many a fierce man that has hoisted many a sail.

On this blessed night of beer, drinks and fights which can make my phone ring to open a door that was closed with a clink.

It still saddens me to think once back on the ship it is maybe a man short. This dangerous job! Claimed by the sea!

Oh we hoist and hoist until the memory turns to fog yet in the clear there is no comfort but the time it takes to past.

Then finally one day comes the heart felt laugh that makes all but the day. Full steam ahead SIG, EDGAR, JOHNATHAN, and PHIL AND SONS.

KEEP ON NARRATING MIKE .   SEE YOU AROUND SOON!

TO THE MEN OF THE MOST DANGEROUS CATCH LOST AT SEA

THE END

www.ingramcontent.com/pod-product-compliance
Lightning Source LLC
Chambersburg PA
CBHW081245170526
45165CB00009B/3211